SOAR 2 SUCCESS
WITH YOUR
EMAIL MARKETING

55 Tips to Drastic Online Results
for your Business

**By
Elizabeth
McCormick
&
Toni
Harris**

©2014 Soar 2 Success International, LLC.
And Toni Harris

Published by Soar 2 Success Publishing
Soar2successPublishing.com

All rights reserved. Except as permitted as under the U.S. Copyright Act of 1976, no part of this publication may be reproduced, distributed, or transmitted in any form or by any means, or stored in a database or retrieval system, without the prior written permission of the authors.

ISBN: 9781943043026

Book Design by Chris Mendoza
chrisdmendoza.com

A Note from Toni

Thank you for picking up this book to learn how to achieve drastic results in your business with email marketing.

I know for some of you this is a drastic step way outside your comfort zone. I applaud you for being willing to take the first step to grow your business. The bottom line is if you don't market your business, then you will be out of business.

I encourage you to read through these tips, then, apply to your business. Implementing one tip at a time will make a HUGE difference in your bottom line. It's up to you to make the time to get started and watch your results SOAR!

Here's to your success!

Toni :)

Special Note

Toni is an expert in Email Marketing as a representative for Constant Contact, the #1 Email Service Provider in the world.

The tips that are given in this book are general and available in most email marketing service providers.

If your provider doesn't have my recommended feature, then contact Toni to get you switched to Constant Contact.

Contact Toni at

DrasticOnlineResults.com

Table of Contents

Section	Tips	Page Range
Email Marketing Basics	Tip #1-7	Page 1-7
Getting Started	Tip #8-11	Page 8-11
Growing Your List	Tip #12-21	Page 12-21
Content is King	Tip #22-31	Page 22-31
Video and Image Marketing	Tip #32-41	Page 32-41
Email + Social Media	Tip #42-48	Page 42-48
Using Reporting Tools	Tip #49-54	Page 49-54
A Final Word from Toni	Tip #55	Page 55

Dedication

This book is dedicated to all the small business owners and entrepreneurs who want to take steps outside of their comfort zone to receive drastic results in their business.

A Note from Elizabeth

How are your clients and potential clients keeping you top of mind? Email marketing is a great way to do this.

Before I was a professional motivational speaker, I was a contract sales trainer specializing in the integration of social media and technology tools to inspire business growth. As the Author and Publisher of the Soar 2 Success Series, I saw a need for training on email marketing. Too many are not doing it "right" and it's impacting their business… But to deliver the very best and most current content for you, our reader, I brought in one of the BEST in the US- Toni Harris.

Together we've de-mystifying the best practices for you in this email marketing guide.

Soar 2 Success- YOUR Way,

Elizabeth McCormick

Email Marketing Basics
Tip #1

Why Email?

The answer is simple. Everyone has email. Not only do they use email, most people check their email *ALL DAY, EVERYDAY!*

If you're not reaching people where they are, online AND in email, your business is INVISIBLE to them.

Your name, your message and your business needs to be where your people are, in their EMAIL.

Email Marketing Basics
Tip #2

Do it Right!

Many business owners shortcut their email marketing by sending what is often called "bootleg" emails.

"Bootleg" emails are where you send the email to yourself and use the Blind CC (bcc): for your audience.

I know you think you are protecting their privacy. However, this is considered SPAM and is actually against the law in the United States.

If this is your method of email marketing, STOP IT NOW! It could cost you.

EMAIL MARKETING BASICS
TIP #3

THE FTC CAN-SPAM ACT
business.ftc.gov

This act gives the guidelines that all email marketers must follow. One of the notable guidelines is:

Your audience must have a way to Opt out or Unsubscribe from your list

If your audience can't opt out, then you are in violation of the Act and the fine can be up to $16,000 per email. PER EMAIL PER OCCURRENCE!

It's not worth sending a bootlegged email!

Email Marketing Basics
Tip #4

More on The FTC CAN-SPAM Act

An additional and important item to note
that is also required is:
A physical address in your email

Some business owners that work out of their home or are "road warriors" may use a PO BOX for privacy.

A PO Box violates this law. It must be a physical address! If you are uncomfortable with your home address going out on every email then consider a workspace share center, like Regus.com or your local UPS or Mail Boxes Etc. Store (or local equivalents) where the rented box comes up as a physical address and is compliant within this law.

EMAIL MARKETING BASICS
Tip #5

SPAM

The reason the CAN-SPAM law was brought to lawmakers is because many were abusing email, some fraudulently.

When you're online it is your responsibility to be aware of SPAMMING activity and not take part in it.

You may be tempted to buy a list or to use someone else's list. DON'T!
This is considered spamming and ultimately results in less engagements and sales. Concentrate on building a permission-based list where your audience agreed to engage with you. Otherwise, spamming can result in serious trouble where you could be "black-listed" from email.

Email Marketing Basics
Tip #6

Avoid SPAM Talk!

If you don't want your emails to resemble SPAM
then avoid common tactics spammers' use:

- ★ Excessive punctuation!!!!
- ★ ALL CAPITAL LETTERS
- ★ No or misleading From: line
- ★ Overuse of $$$ or other symbols
- ★ Avoid use of "FREE" or "Click here"

Most email marketing service providers include as part of their service a check for CAN-SPAM compliance and will electronically review your email draft before it is sent to ensure your email doesn't end up in the junk folder.

Email Marketing Basics
Tip #7

What does a service cost?

Email Marketing Service Providers vary in services and cost. Do some research, ask around, and connect with Toni to get your questions answered.

But here is a more relevant question to ask:

What will NOT using a service cost you?

Between the CAN-SPAM Law, the SPAM filters, and the added value of branding, scheduled delivery times, and the ability to reach the masses with the click of a button, email marketing is an excellent return on investment.

GETTING STARTED
TIP #8

SUBJECT LINES MATTER

Use the 3 "S's" of subject lines:

Short
Surprise/Shock
Simple

A good subject line tells the reader the benefit of opening the email, not just what it is.

Download a list of sample subject lines at:

Soar2Success.com/email-marketing-subject-lines

Getting Started
Tip #9

Branding

Your emails are a way to increase exposure to your brand.

Make sure your template reflects you and your brand.

Ideally, you want your email template to match your website.

This allows your audience to have a better experience when clicking through between the newsletter and the website. It builds trust because they visually know it's YOU!

Getting Started
Tip #10
Who is the Email From?

Being recognizable in your audience's mailbox is important. 60% of people determine whether they will open an email by who it is from. Make sure you use a personal or company name (preferably both) your audience will recognize.

If they don't know whom the email is from, it won't get opened.

And you WANT your emails opened.

Getting Started
Tip #11

Know the "purpose" of your emails- for your client

What's in it for them?

They need to know the value you are going to provide.
Which means you need to know this value,
so you can communicate it!

Is it cost-saving opportunities?
Tips?
Recipes
Sharing content?

What can you offer that your clients (and potential clients) want?

_____

_____

GROWING YOUR LIST
TIP #12

JUST ASK

In order for you to achieve drastic results in your business, growing your lists is essential.

With online and e-commerce the saying is the, "The Money is in the list" and the "list is worth gold".

While meeting new people, ask your new acquaintance:

"Do you mind if I add you to my monthly newsletter list for *[cost savings, ideas, recipes, new products, training-what's in it for them]*?"

Give them an idea of what they will receive and how often, most people will say yes. Then, they'll be looking for it.

Growing Your List
Tip #13

Put "Join my list" on your Print Marketing

On your business cards, postcards, fliers, brochures, etc. **educate** your clients and prospects how they can join your list.

As an example, to join Toni's list, text **drasticsteps** to **22828**. (Go ahead, pick up your cell phone and join Toni's list now!)

To join Elizabeth's List and receive 30- 3 minute training videos to lead yourself in life and business:

Soar2Success.com/leadership-challenge

Growing Your List
Tip #14

Use Facebook to Grow Your List

On your Fan page, put "Join My List" instructions in your status.

Put it in your cover photo

Some email marketing service providers even have an application to work within Facebook to encourage enrollments.

This is typically an advanced skill. It's OK to hire help.

GROWING YOUR LIST
TIP #15

POINT OF SALE

Just about every time we make a purchase, online or in a store, we are asked for our email address.

These retailers are growing their lists.

Why don't you do the same?

Every time you make a sale, ask your customer for their email to add to your list.

Don't forget to tell them why it's to their benefit!

Growing Your List
Tip #16

QR Codes are COOL!

Use a QR Code to get people to Scan-to-Join your list.

Better yet, have it put on the shoulder or back of a T-shirt and have your family and employees wear them all over town!

Growing Your List
Tip #17

Collaborate

Conduct a joint training, live event, webinar or a telesummit with other people who have lists. Who do you know that has a list that serves the same customers you serve? Look for synergy!

When their audience registers for the event, you can add the registrants to your list. This is an implied permission and perfectly acceptable.

This is also a great way to keep your list fresh.

Growing Your List
Tip #18

Target Your List

Keep your lists segregated by customers, prospects, or in various categories. This will help you to effectively market to the right lists at the right time. This way you can target your marketing to the right people at the right time.

Create separate lists for different categories.

Some ideas are:
Type Of Customer
Spending patterns/Previous Purchase item
Potential Customers
Gender for targeted marketing messaging
Where they originated from- online versus in person etc...

GROWING YOUR LIST
TIP #19

UNSUBSCRIBES ARE GOOD

Don't take it personal when someone unsubscribes from your list. They typically unsubscribe for their own reasons.

When people unsubscribe they are doing you a favor. It's helping you stay clear s to who is interested in staying informed, knowing this information can be helpful to you when creating content that is targeted for your list.

So don't cry over unsubscribes,
just keep building your list.

Growing Your List
Tip #20

Use your existing list in Yahoo, Gmail, Hotmail, Outlook, etc.

These people already know you so you could jumpstart your list with their email addresses.

Send them a ONE TO ONE email first (Yes, to each person):

- ★ Announcing your new marketing strategy
- ★ Why they should be on your list
- ★ Providing your opt in link to join your list

Create the email in a document to cut and paste over to each recipient.

GROWING YOUR LIST
TIP #21

GO MOBILE

Download the list capturing app for your email service provider on your mobile device and capture email addresses as you are networking.

Many of the email marketing services have an app for your phone.

Have you checked?

Go to the APP Store or Google Marketplace and search.

Content Is King
Tip #22

Less is More!

Keep your newsletter and other content short.
If your newsletter is longer than an
8 ½ x 11 sheet of paper then it's too long.

Often, the person receiving the email may not even scroll down, so ensure your most important info is in the top ½ of the page.

Remember, if you have more to say,
you can give them a link to your website.

Content is King
Tip #23

O.P.C. (Other People's Content)

Your content does not need to be original, just interesting.

You can use content that is specifically created
for use in marketing communications.

Google the words "PLR – Private Label Rights"
to see the variety of OPC that is available.

PLR is a license where the author sells most or all
of the intellectual property rights to their work.

What websites did you find that offer PLR material?

_____

_____

Content is King
Tip #24

Repurpose and Reuse

You can also reuse your own content.

Have you written newsletters in the past?
What about positive thoughts on social media?
Do you have blog posts on your website?
Content pages or product pages on your website?

Those can be repurposed and reused too. This is the place to tease it and send them to where YOU want them.
Drive them to an action of your choosing.

Content is King
Tip #25

Be the Expert and Tell Us What You Know…

The mistake many of us make is that we think because we know something, everyone else knows it too. Nothing can be further from the truth. Be the expert! Tell us what you know about your product and your industry. Enlighten us on how what you know can improve our lives, then we are happy to engage with you.

What do you know that your audience doesn't?
What is the history? What is your story?

_____

_____

_____

Content is King
Tip #26

Don't Overly Self Promote!

Buy, buy, BUY?

No one wants to be bombarded with this message. But if you show yourself as the expert with your content and knowledgeable about your industry, then your audience will buy your products and services because of YOU and your brand.

80-20 Rule (Pareto's Principle) applies here.
80% of your content should be informative
No more than 20% "salesy" in nature

Don't be too pushy and the sales will come.

Content is King
Tip #27

CALL TO ACTION

Make sure your message has a distinct call to action.

Tell your audience what you want them to do and how you want them to respond. If you want them to register for your event, make sure the register button is clear.

Also, put your call to action above the scroll line to capture their attention immediately.

Download a list of "call to actions" at

Soar2Sucess.com/email-marketing-call-to-action

Content is King
Tip #28

Link Back to Your Website

<u>CLICK HERE</u>   <u>LEARN MORE</u>
<u>CONNECT WITH ME</u>   <u>SEE MORE</u>   <u>MORE INFO</u>
<u>GO TO MY WEBSITE</u>

Make sure you use links throughout the newsletter that link back to your website.

All images should be linked to your website.

Did you know text links are clicked more often than picture links so make sure you include text AND graphic links throughout your newsletter.

Content is King
Tip #29

An Audio says 10,000 Words

Use audio to engage with your audience.

Record your own sound bites-
you can even do this with your mobile phone!

And link them to your emails for your
audience to download or listen live.

With the world being more mobile, using audio allows for
instant engagement and showcases you as the expert.

Watch for info on Video in the next section!

Content is King
Tip #30

Know When to Send

To get the maximum engagement from your audience, when to send is important.

If your business is not a weekend business, then don't send an email on Friday afternoon.

Wait and schedule it for Monday or Tuesday when your audience may be less busy.

The bottom line is you must know your audience and the best day and time to send to your lists.

What are your best times:

Content is King
Tip #31

Help Your Audience and They Will Help You

If your audience sees value in your content,
they will share you with their friends.

Make it easy for them by:

★ Keeping your content short and sweet

★ Be informative

★ Give away something of value,
a reason to share the email

★ Help them to clearly see "what's in it for them"
to engage with you

Video and Image Marketing
Tip #32

Pictures Say a 1,000 Words- Still!

The more pictures you can use to
convey your message the better.

Pictures allow your audience to instantly connect
with you, your brand, and your product.

Pictures draw them in.

Help them visualize your message. Don't get so bogged
down with the text that you forget the pictures.

Video and Image Marketing
Tip #33

Videos say 10,000 Words!

More powerful than pictures is VIDEO.

Videos are the hottest marketing tool around!

Videos add impact and allow the audience to see the real you.
Yes- YOU! Your personality shines, your message resonates
and this builds trust with your audience.

Begin using videos consistently now and
you could see drastic results.

VIDEO AND IMAGE MARKETING
TIP #34

MORE INTERACTION WITH YOUR AUDIENCE

If you want more interaction between you and your
audience use videos, photos and photo albums
to boost your social media posts:

Videos = 100% more engagement
Photos = 120% more engagement
Albums = 180% more engagement

Visual Media works. Start thinking visually.

Source:
http://bit.ly/email_interaction page 3

Video and Image Marketing
Tip #35

Testimonials

Place testimonials from your customers in your newsletter.

It's one thing for you to say you are great;
however, it's better if your customers say you are great.

Ask your customers to give you 30 seconds
to a minute of video testimonial.

This will get amazing results for your business!

Make a list of customers who would give you a testimonial:

Can be taken with your cell phone, use your phone
to shoot video horizontally.

Video and Image Marketing
Tip #36

Use Video to Educate

Use video to teach your audience something.

Showcase your expertise. Show off a little!

Prepare a 3 to 5 minute video on your mobile phone or tablet to educate your audience.

What can you teach your audience in a short video?

_____

_____

_____

VIDEO AND IMAGE MARKETING
TIP #37

MAKE IMAGES CLICKABLE

On average, 67% of email recipients
don't see images right away.*

Some email providers don't allow the images
to be seen when the emails are first opened.

Make your images clickable to drive traffic to your website
or social media sites, then customize with a written
description of that image or video.

Source:
* *http://bit.ly/sherpablog*

VIDEO AND IMAGE MARKETING
TIP #38

CREATE A YOUTUBE CHANNEL

YouTube is a valuable resource to show your talents. And YouTube is its own search engine, so be sure to add descriptions and a link in the description to join your mailing list.

You can upload your own videos, product demonstrations and testimonials. Set up your YouTube videos to automatically share on your social media platforms and share them in your email marketing too! It really is easy you just have to do it!

Download an instruction sheet on
how to create your own channel:

Soar2Success.com/email-marketing-YouTubeVideo

Image Marketing
Tip #39

Create a Commercial

Use some of the video creation programs such as Windows Movie Maker, Powerpoint (using Save as video), Animoto.com (fee applies), Vine.com to create your own video commercials.

Load on video social sharing sites such as: YouTube, Vine.com, Viddler.com, Vimeo.com, Dailymotion.com

Or invest with a professional video production company for a commercial. There are solutions for every budget.

Then share the links in your email marketing campaigns and on social media sites.

Video and Image Marketing
Tip #40

Create a Photo Album of You and Your Business

A photo album shared in your email and social media marketing can get you exposure all over the world.

Start taking more pictures.

Try different angles.

Take a photo with your customers,
of you in your business in action.

Add a quote from a customer over the photo, a statistic about your business, a business tip, or a quote from you.

Video and Image Marketing
Tip #41

Photos + Videos = WOW!

Combining your business photos with your videos
can grow your business exponentially!

Toni and Elizabeth both have gotten many speaking
engagements because from sharing videos
in emails and social media.

Do the same and watch your business **SOAR!**

S2S with your Email Marketing

EMAIL & SOCIAL MEDIA
TIP #42

WHY GO SOCIAL?

Over 1 billion users on Facebook*

Over 288 million users on Twitter**

71% of people are more likely to purchase if referred by a friend through social media***

Source:
**Facebook (2012)*
**Global Web Index (February 2013)
***Hubspot (January 2012)

Email & Social Media
Tip #43

Encourage Your Audience to Share YOU on Their Social Media Sites

When sending an email blast don't forget to include the icons that allow your audience to share your newsletter on their Facebook, Twitter, LinkedIn and Pinterest accounts.

Need artwork for these icons?

Go to *iconfinder.com* for free options to download social media icons in different styles.

Now that's exploding your brand!

Email & Social Media
Tip #44

Repurpose Your Content From Newsletter into Social Media

Take snippets from your past email newsletters and place them on social media for maximum engagement.

After all, you've already written it.
Why not use it again and share it.

This way your social media audience gets to experience how smart you are!

Email & Social Media
Tip #45

Share and Share Alike!

Ask your Facebook Friends if you can share your newsletters and other posts on their Facebook page.

Most will say absolutely! Get their permission and be willing to reciprocate and allow their shares on yours. Some groups even have a "share day".

Once they say yes, click the Share button in Facebook; choose their timeline and share!

Now their friends will see you too!

HINT! Don't ask them to do it for you. While their intentions are good, they may forget. Make it easy on them!

Email & Social Media
Tip #46

Make it EASY for Referrals

By including a "forward to a friend" icon in your emails, your audience can easily forward this to their friends.

Picture it…
they forward it to a friend and their friend
engages with you too!

Priceless!

Email & Social Media
Tip #47

Join My List Button

Join My Mailing List

Make sure your newsletter has a "join my mailing list" button.

When your email is forwarded by a friend, or shared on social media, then their friends can join your list.

Many email services include this button for placement into the email for you.

Email & Social Media
Tip #48

Share Other People's Information on Your Social Media

If you want people to play in your sandbox, you have to play in theirs too.

So start sharing the newsletters and social media posts of your followers.

When you do unto them, they will be happy to do unto you too.

GIVE FIRST! USING REPORTING TOOLS
TIP #49

SOCIAL CAMPAIGNS

Use a social campaign program or Facebook developer program to get more LIKES and engagement on your Facebook social media.

This program allows you to give away an item, discount, create a contest, or other promotion in exchange for Likes.

It's a great tool to grow your social media presence and increase your interactions.

What could you offer?

Using Reporting Tools
Tip #50

Automatically Send your Emails to Social Media

Many email-marketing providers offer a sharing service where your email is automatically shared when it sends out.

When scheduling your email marketing, use this sharing service (e.g. Simple Share in Constant Contact) to share your emails in social media.

These emails go to Facebook, Twitter and LinkedIn as soon as they hit the audience's mailbox. And this increases the opportunities for your audience to share and do business with you.

Using Reporting Tools
Tip #51

Who Opened My Email?

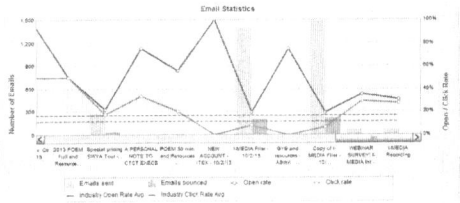

The real value of using an email service provider is the ability to see who opened your email, the date, the time, if they clicked a link, if they forwarded the email, etc.

Used correctly, these statistics can really tell you where to target your marketing.

Using Reporting Tools
Tip #52

Tracking Your Open Rates

A good open rate is 20-30%.

Don't worry if your open rates aren't as high as you first expected.

Even if your audience doesn't open your email they still see you "waving hello" at them in their Inbox. You are also letting them know that you are still "open for business".

Keep sending emails- seeing you "waving hello" will keep you top of mind when they have a need your business can service.

Using Reporting Tools
Tip #53

Are They Clicking My Links?

There are reports showing you how many clicked your links, and WHO clicked your links.

This information can be invaluable for future emails, in deciding whom to follow up with on a phone call and in determining what is working and what's not. Then adjust.

Use this information to create smaller more targeted lists.

When using an email marketing service, reports like this are valuable. Ensure you are reviewing your reports on a regular basis.

Using Reporting Tools
Tip #54

Manage Your Bounces

What is a Bounce?
When an email cannot get through due to a bad address, a typo, a vacation reply, a full inbox, or email "no longer in service" it bounces back to your email service provider and YOU.

Check your bounces list to make sure there are no typos on your lists.

Correct the emails that bounce back so that no one misses out on your good information.

If you see their email is not getting through, this can be your call list. It's your opportunity to connect with them and get a good email address!

A Final Word from Toni
Tip #55

Thank Your Audience

Pay attention to those who support you.

Thank your audience for sharing your messages.

Thank your audience for forwarding your emails.

Thank them for their continued engagement on social media.

Simply put, say,

"Thank You!"

Other titles in the Soar 2 Success Series

Find More Online at
Soar2SuccessBooks.com

Other titles in the Soar 2 Success Series

Find More Online at
Soar2SuccessBooks.com

Other titles in the Soar 2 Success Series

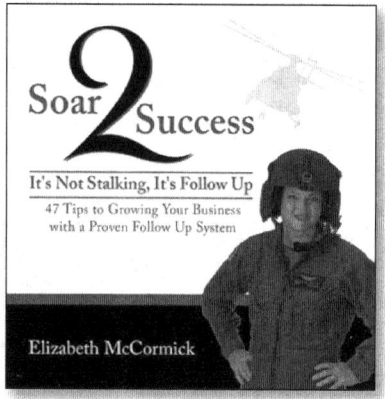

Find More Online at
Soar2SuccessBooks.com

Other titles in the Soar 2 Success Series

Find More Online at
Soar2SuccessBooks.com

Other titles in the Soar 2 Success Series

Find More Online at
Soar2SuccessBooks.com

Other titles in the Soar 2 Success Series

Find More Online at
Soar2SuccessBooks.com

Other titles in the Soar 2 Success Series

Find More Online at
Soar2SuccessBooks.com

Other titles in the Soar 2 Success Series

Find More Online at
Soar2SuccessBooks.com

Other titles in the Soar 2 Success Series

Find More Online at
Soar2SuccessBooks.com

Other titles in the Soar 2 Success Series

Find More Online at
Soar2SuccessBooks.com

About Toni Harris

As an entrepreneur for over 20 years, Toni has experienced the good, the bad and the ugly of entrepreneurship. As a Constant Contact Solution Provider, she received the "Rookie of the Year" award for her outstanding performance. Toni specializes in email and social media marketing coaching her small business clients to achieve drastic results in their businesses to increase revenue and profitability.

Affectionately known as "The Turnaround Queen®," Toni is a passionate, dynamic and energetic speaker who "wows" her audiences melding best practices with real world solutions.

BOOK TONI
FOR YOUR NEXT MEETING OR TRAINING EVENT.

CONTACT TONI ABOUT EMAIL MARKETING AT:

info@DrasticOnlineResults.com
DrasticOnlineResults.com

Connect with Toni On Social Media at:

Facebook.com/drasticsteps
Twitter.com/toniharrisspeak
Linkedin.com/in/toniharrisspeak
Youtube.com/toniharrisspeak

About Elizabeth McCormick

Elizabeth shattered the glass ceiling in the military as an Army Black Hawk Pilot, then in her corporate career as a global contract negotiator. And now she continues to rain glass as an in demand International Motivational Speaker and CEO of Soar 2 Success International.

As a decorated U.S. Army Black Hawk Helicopter Pilot, Elizabeth flew missions such as Air Assault/Rappelling, Command & Control, VIP, and Military intelligence. She supported United Nations peacekeeping operations in Kosovo, receiving the Meritorious Service Medal for her excellence in service, and in 2011 Elizabeth was awarded the Congressional Veteran Commendation.

Elizabeth is a founding member of the John Maxwell Team of speakers, coaches and trainers, and a dynamic energizing entertainer inspiring audiences worldwide.

MORE ABOUT ELIZABETH MCCORMICK

A frequent face in the media, Elizabeth has been seen on ABC, CBS, NBC, FOX News, in the Wall Street Journal and more. A No. 1 best-selling author, her personal development book, *The P.I.L.O.T. Method*, is a "must read!"

Text **SOAR to 96000** to receive free video training.

BOOK ELIZABETH TO SPEAK AT YOUR NEXT EVENT:

PilotSpeaker.com
BlackHawk@PilotSpeaker.com
Linkedin.com/in/PilotSpeaker
Twitter.com/PilotSpeaker
Facebook.com/BlackHawkPilot

ABOUT SOAR 2 SUCCESS INTERNATIONAL

Soar 2 Success International LLC, bringing excellence through experience. Founded in 2012, Soar 2 Success International has rapidly grown to be a premier speaking and training company representing high quality professional speakers.

Soar 2 Success added a Publishing division in 2013 bringing you the control and rights of self-publishing with the guidance and processes of a traditional publishing house.

Find Speakers, Books and Publishing information at:

Soar2Success.com

Connect with us at:

Facebook.com/soar2success
Twitter.com/soar2successint